Creature

Monkeys

Tracey Crawford

Heinemann
LIBRARY

www.heinemann.co.uk/library
Visit our website to find out more information about Heinemann Library books.

To order:
☎ Phone 44 (0) 1865 888066
Send a fax to 44 (0) 1865 314091
📄 Visit the Heinemann Bookshop at www.heinemann.co.uk/library to browse our
💻 catalogue and order online.

First published in Great Britain by Heinemann Library,
Halley Court, Jordan Hill, Oxford OX2 8EJ, part of Harcourt
Education. Heinemann is a registered trademark of Harcourt
Education Ltd.

Editorial: Tracey Crawford, Cassie Mayer, Dan Nunn,
and Sarah Chappelow
Design: Jo Hinton-Malivoire
Picture Research: Tracy Cummins and Tracey Engel
Production: Duncan Gilbert

Originated by Chroma Graphics (Overseas) Pte. Ltd
Printed and bound in China by South China
Printing Company

ISBN 978 0 431 18223 0 (hardback)
11 10 09 08 07
10 9 8 7 6 5 4 3 2 1

ISBN 978 0 431 18346 6 (paperback)
12 11 10 09 08
10 9 8 7 6 5 4 3 2 1

British Library Cataloguing in Publication Data
Crawford, Tracey
    Monkeys. - (Creature comparisons)
    1.Monkeys - Juvenile literature
    I.Title
    599.8

Acknowledgements
The publishers would like to thank the following for permission
to reproduce photographs: Corbis pp. 4 (bird, Arthur Morris),
5 (Frank Lukasseck/zefa), 10 (Gallo Images), 15 (Darrell Gulin),
18 (Philip Marazzi; Papilio), 19 (Keren Su), 20 (Tom Brakefield),
22 (Macaque monkeys, Yann Arthus-Bertrand); T. Falotico,
ETHOCEBUS p. 22 (Capuchin monkey); Getty Images pp. 4 (fish),
6 (Michael Nichols), 9 (Peter Lillie), 11 (John Bracegirdle), 13 (Brian
Kenney), 16 (Art Wolfe), 21 (Eastcott Momatiuk); Naturepl.com
pp. 7 (Pete Oxford), 14 (XI ZHI NONG), 17; Shutterstock p. 12
(Brian Tan); Carlton Ward p. 4 (snake, frog).

Cover photograph of a black howler monkey reproduced with
permission of Nature Picture Library/Anup Shah and an emperor
tamarin reproduced with permission of Corbis/Theo Allofs. Back
cover photograph of a monkey in the rainforest reproduced with
permission of Corbis/Philip Marazzi, Papilio.

Every effort has been made to contact copyright holders of any
material reproduced in this book. Any omissions will be rectified in
subsequent printings if notice is given to the publishers.

Contents

There are many types of animals.

Monkeys are one type of animal.
Monkeys are mammals.

All monkeys have fur.

All monkeys can climb.

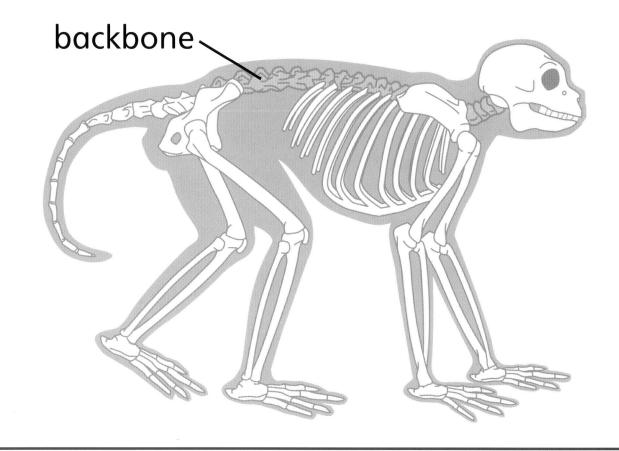

backbone

All monkeys have a backbone.

All baby monkeys get milk
from their mother.

Most monkeys have a tail.

But these monkeys do not.

Most monkeys have thumbs.

But this monkey does not.

Most monkeys live in trees.

But these monkeys do not.

Some monkeys are big.

Some monkeys are small.

Some monkeys live in warm places.

Some monkeys live in cold places.

Every monkey is different.

Every monkey is special.

Monkey facts

These monkeys live where it is cold. They sit in warm water to keep warm.

Monkeys are very clever. This monkey uses a stone as a tool. It hammers a nut with a stone to open it.

Picture glossary

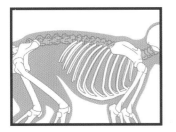 **backbone** the part of the skeleton that goes from the head to the tail

Index

Notes to parents and teachers
Before reading
Talk to the children about monkeys. Has anyone seen a monkey on television or in a zoo? Have they heard the expression "You little monkey"? Why might someone say that to a child?

After reading
Play the "Like a monkey game" (based on Simon Says). Give the children instructions to act like a monkey, e.g. monkey climb, monkey crouch, monkey run, monkey swing. Occasionally give the instruction without saying "Monkey". Any child who does the action is out.
Say the traditional rhyme: "I went to the animal fair. The birds and the beasts were there. The big baboon, by the light of the moon, Was combing his auburn hair. The monkey fell out of his bunk. And slid down the elephant's trunk. The elephant sneezed and fell on his knees. And what became of the monkey, monkey, monkey, monkey, monkey, monkey."